Lucille Ball

A Little Golden Book® Biography

By Wendy Loggia

Illustrated by Chin Ko

The author dedicates this book to her hometown of Jamestown, New York.

A GOLDEN BOOK • NEW YORK

Text copyright © 2022 by Wendy Loggia
Cover art and interior illustrations copyright © 2022 by Chin Ko
All rights reserved. Published in the United States by Golden Books, an imprint of
Random House Children's Books, a division of Penguin Random House LLC, 1745 Broadway,
New York, NY 10019. Golden Books, A Golden Book, A Little Golden Book, the G colophon,
and the distinctive gold spine are registered trademarks of Penguin Random House LLC.
rhcbooks.com
Educators and librarians, for a variety of teaching tools, visit us at RHTeachersLibrarians.com
Library of Congress Control Number: 2021947497
ISBN 978-0-593-48264-3 (trade) — ISBN 978-0-593-48265-0 (ebook)
Printed in the United States of America
10 9 8 7 6 5 4 3

Lucille Désirée Ball was born in her grandparents' apartment on August 6, 1911, in Jamestown, New York.

When Lucy was three, her father died of typhoid fever. Lucy never forgot the day she learned the sad news. But a few months later came some good news: her mother, DeDe, gave birth to Lucy's brother, Freddy.

From the beginning, little Lucy loved attention. At the grocery store, she liked to hop up onto the counter and pretend to be a frog. Customers would give her pennies and candy!

Lucy's grandfather bought a house for the whole family to live in next to Chautauqua Lake. From her bedroom window, Lucy could see a hedge of purple lilacs. Lilacs soon became Lucy's favorite flower. The lake was perfect for swimming and boating in the summer—but boy, was it cold in the winter!

A short walk away was Celoron Park, a place with rides, a boardwalk, a bandstand, and, best of all, a stage. Lucy loved watching performances there and then putting on shows at home with Freddy. When Lucy was a teenager, she worked at the park, selling hamburgers and ice cream. And she performed in plays at her school and in a local theater.

All the while, Lucy dreamed of being an actress.

When Lucy was fifteen, DeDe sent her to acting school in New York City. The school was far from home, so Lucy took a train to the city and lived with family friends while she studied.

It didn't go well. Her teachers made fun of her rural accent and her dancing. They told her she would never be a success. Lucy went home and tried to forget about her dream.

Then Lucy's family had some financial problems and had to move out of their house. Lucy was determined to help, so back to New York she went, to try to get work.

Lucy auditioned for many shows when she was sixteen and seventeen. She was excited to be hired as a chorus girl on Broadway—but was fired soon after because she couldn't do the dance steps. To pay her bills, she dyed her hair and worked at Hattie Carnegie's dress shop, modeling fancy clothes for rich customers. Hattie taught Lucy how to pose.

Then something scary happened—Lucy became very sick. After many months, she was finally strong enough to stand and walk again. But there was a bad surprise: her left leg was now shorter than her right.

Do you think this stopped Lucy? No way!

Lucy kept modeling. She was even on a billboard in Times Square. But Lucy's dream was to act. Her lucky break came when she ran into an agent named Sylvia Hahlo. Sylvia told her an actress had backed out of a new movie and the studio needed someone to replace her. Was Lucy interested?

Lucy didn't think twice. She auditioned.
And she got the job! She was finally on her
way to Hollywood to be a movie star.

Lucy made a lot of movies, but the ones she was in weren't the most popular. They were known as "B" movies. And Lucy became Queen of the B's.

In the 1930s, studios would discover actors and actresses—the "talent"—and sign them to multiyear contracts. This happened to Lucy.

On the set of one of those movies, *Too Many Girls,* Lucy met a handsome young Cuban musician. His name was Desi Arnaz. People thought Lucy and Desi made an odd couple. But they didn't care. They fell in love, got married, and bought a ranch in California.

Lucy and Desi were a great team. They formed a company they named Desilu Productions. They created a vaudeville act together. And then came the news that would change everything: CBS asked Lucy and Desi to make a TV show!

I Love Lucy premiered on October 15, 1951. Lucy and Desi played Lucy and Ricky Ricardo. Lucy was a housewife who wanted to be in show business, and Desi was a bandleader with an orchestra. Their best friends were Ethel and Fred Mertz.

I Love Lucy became the most-watched show on television. No one wanted to miss a single minute. It was so funny! Lucy wore crazy costumes and made silly faces. If something would get a laugh, she'd do it!

Lucy's famous red hair color came from a bottle. She chose red so she would stand out.

It's no surprise that Lucille Ball is also known as the Queen of Comedy. In one episode of her show, Lucy and Ethel get jobs in a candy factory and can't keep up with the conveyor belt. Lucy hides chocolate in her dress—and her mouth!

In another episode, Lucy stomps grapes with her bare feet—and gets into a messy fruit fight!

This was a special time in Lucy's life. Not only was her show a huge success, but she and Desi had a baby girl, Lucie, and then a little boy, Desi Jr., two years later.

I Love Lucy aired for six years. Sadly, after it ended, Lucy and Desi's marriage ended, too. Lucy became the sole owner of Desilu Productions—and the first woman to run a Hollywood studio.

In late 1961, Lucy married a man named Gary Morton. They were happy together. But Lucy and Desi never stopped caring about one another.

Lucy wanted to keep making people laugh. She went on to star in *The Lucy Show* and *Here's Lucy* and in the movie musical *Mame*. She won many awards and received two stars on the Hollywood Walk of Fame.

Lucy died on April 26, 1989. Generations of fans around the world were devastated. One of Hollywood's biggest and most-loved stars was gone.

The Lucy Desi Museum and the National Comedy Center opened in Lucy's hometown of Jamestown. Although Lucy is no longer with us, the laughter and love for her remain.

Lucille Ball was a trailblazer: actress, comedian, studio executive and producer, and Hollywood legend. A small-town girl with big dreams had the courage to chase them—and found success beyond her wildest imagination. That's why everyone loves Lucy!